Canadian Folk Songs for the Young

SELECTED BY

Barbara Cass-Beggs

ILLUSTRATED BY

Debi Perna

Douglas & McIntyre
Vancouver/Toronto

Douglas & McIntyre
585 Bloor Street West
Toronto, Ontario M6G 1K5

Canadian Cataloguing in Publication Data

Main entry under title:

Canadian folk songs for the young : [music]

Rev. ed.
Words and unacc. melodies, most with chord symbols.
Songs in languages other than English are accompanied by
English translations.
Includes commentary.
Includes bibliographical references.
ISBN 0-88894-847-6 (bound) ISBN 1-55054-257-5 (pbk.)

1. Children's songs - Canada. 2. Folk songs - Canada.
I. Cass-Beggs, Barbara, 1904-1990. II. Perna, Debi.

M1678.C346 1992   782.7'42162'00971   C91-092506-8

Design by Michael Solomon
Printed and bound in Hong Kong

CONTENTS

THOSE *of us who work with children realize what an important part music can play in their lives, and how essential it is to provide them with songs which are both enjoyable and musically significant.*

Folk songs merit this description, and in the wide range of available folk songs there are many which appeal to children. Some can be enjoyed by the very young child along with the standard singing games and nursery rhymes—which are, of course, folk songs too.

To define a folk song is a difficult thing to do, because everyone seems to have his or her own definition and all the definitions differ considerably. However, let us start off with "the authorities."

Marius Barbeau, our most outstanding Canadian folk song collector and founder of the Canadian Folk Music Society, says: "What characterizes ancient folk songs is their inveterate nomadism. Born under the stars, as it were, they at once took to the road or the sea. . . . Impelled by a fate that goes back to their oral birth and transmission, far away and long ago, they had to keep on travelling. . . . To the songs, all of Europe was one country, which they criss-crossed in all directions. Often they embarked on ships and sailed the seas, landing at many ports even in America."[1]

Cecil Sharp, England's most renowned folk song collector and writer, has writ- *ten an entire book devoted to defining what he considers to be the true characteristics of a folk song. He introduces* English Folk Song: Some Conclusions *with a very short definition which is worth quoting as a summary of his thinking: "In this book the word folk-song will be used exclusively to denote the song which has been created by the common people, in contradistinction to the song, popular or otherwise, which has been composed by the educated."*[2]

Since a folk song is passed along orally and added to by many different people, it is well summed up by Vaughan Williams as "an air with variations."[3] *He goes on to agree with Cecil Sharp and Marius Barbeau that although the original air of a folk tune is made up by an individual, the music has a communal evolution as well as the words.*

In order to survive, folk songs had to be enjoyable and musically significant. Enjoyable because they deal with everyday happenings which interest children: boat building; fishing; dancing; making up nonsense rhymes because one is happy. Musically significant because, while conveying history and custom, these songs possess lively rhythms and simple but beautiful melodies.

Because this book is directed to Canadian children (although it is hoped that children from other countries will enjoy it too) the selected folk songs are all

Canadian, for it is important for children to know their own songs first in order to discover their roots. According to American folk singer Alan Lomax, "The first function of music, especially folk music, is to produce a feeling of security for the listener by voicing the particular quality of a land and the life of its people. . . . Folk song calls the native back to his roots and prepares him emotionally to dance, worship, work, fight, or make love in ways normal to his place."[4]

With so many folk song books already available it may well be asked, "Why one more?" The fact is that the songs which children can enjoy most are scattered in many books, and unless one has a fairly wide knowledge of children and folk songs it is not easy to select them. And such a selection needs editing—not to censor, but to ensure that the children can understand what they sing.

Collectors preserve our songs by recording them in books and storing them in archives, but unless they are sung, songs do not truly live, and our children will not be aware of their Canadian heritage. Canadian children must be given the opportunity of acquiring a taste for their forefathers' songs. They can then move on to absorb and enjoy the remarkable variety and beauty of folk songs from other parts of the world.

Folk song on this continent is, in Alan Lomax's words, a museum of musical antiques from many lands. Canada's original folk songs were of course Native and Inuit, but we have inherited songs from our founding cultures— the French and British—and from the

many other cultural groups which go to form the Canadian mosaic. In addition, a certain number of songs such as "I'se the B'y" and "Flunky Jim" are indigenous.

Having taught our songs to a succession of school children, I have only included in this book those songs which they have obviously enjoyed and wanted to sing again.

Because it is interesting to know the background of the songs, there are brief notes on them which it is hoped will be read or interpreted to the children.

In general, folk songs are better unaccompanied, except perhaps for handclaps or drum beat. However, in some instances it is fun to use a guitar or autoharp, so some simple chording has been included.

The book is divided into three parts, and although children may want to sing songs from all three sections, Part One is particularly suitable for the pre-school and kindergarten level, Part Two to the younger grades and Part Three to older children.

My thanks go to all those who have collected these songs. I am particularly indebted to Edith Fowke, whose scholarly notes have provided the historical background material for much of my text. And thanks to Kristine and Liza Palin for helping me to choose these songs.

1 Marius Barbeau, *Folk Songs of Old Quebec*, National Museum of Canada.
2 Cecil Sharp, *English Folk Song: Some Conclusions*, Methuen and Company Ltd., London, England.
3 R. Vaughan Williams, *National Music and Other Essays*, Oxford University Press, Oxford, England.
4 Alan Lomax, *The Folk Songs of North America*, Doubleday and Company, Inc., New York, U.S.A.

Acadian Lullaby

This very beautiful lullaby comes from the Maritime provinces. It was sung to Helen Creighton by a woman who lives in the village of Pubuico. The song goes back to the time of the French who settled in these parts and who were called Acadians.

With its pentatonic (5 note) pattern, "Acadian Lullaby" is easily sung to solfa, or played on a xylophone, chime bars, or the black notes of the piano. It is also very easily accompanied with other notes or combination of notes from the pentatonic scale.

Dors, dors, le p'tit bi-bi. C'est le beau p'tit bi - bi à ma-ma.
Sleep, sleep, lit-tle ba -by. You're such a love-ly Mo-ther's lit-tle one.

Dors, dors, dors, dors, Dors, dors, le bi - bi à ma-ma. De-
Sleep, sleep, sleep, sleep, Sleep, sleep, Mo-ther's ba - by. To-

main s'y fait beau j'-irons au grand-père. Dors, dors le p' - tit bi-bi.
mor-row if it's fine we will see Grand-pa. Sleep, sleep, lit-tle ba - by.

Dors, dors, dors, dors, Dors, le beau p' - tit bi- bi à ma-ma.
Sleep, sleep, sleep, sleep, Sleep, love-ly one, Mo-ther's lit-tle ba - by.

Dors, dors, le p'tit bibi.
C'est le beau p'tit bibi à mama.
Dors, dors, dors, dors,
Dors, dors, le bibi à mama.
Demain s'y fait beau j'irons au grand-père.
Dors, dors, le p'tit bibi.
Dors, dors, dors, dors,
Dors, le beau p'tit bibi à mama.

Sleep, sleep, little baby.
You're such a lovely Mother's little one.
Sleep, sleep, sleep, sleep,
Sleep, sleep, Mother's baby.
Tomorrow if it's fine we will see Grandpa.
Sleep, sleep, little baby.
Sleep, sleep, sleep, sleep,
Sleep, lovely one, Mother's little baby.

Ah! Si mon moine voulait danser

This happy dance tune, which originally described all the things a young lady would give a monk (*moine*) if only he would dance, was sung by the French voyageurs and the early habitants in New France. The French words seem to suggest that the monk's inattention to the sound of the mill wheel is part of his inability or unwillingness to dance—that is, he lacks a sense of rhythm. (Of course, this may be reading a fairly subtle idea into the words.)

Because *moine* can mean "top" as well as "monk," the children soon began to sing this tune as they whipped their tops. Here are some top-whipping words as well as the original

French words. It is such an infectious tune that the children may want to sing it often to various sets of words, including those about a merry-go-round.

When the children sing "The Top" version of this song, they can pretend to whip tops. Similarly, when they sing "The Merry-Go-Round" they can move in a circle, pretending to be on horses on a merry-go-round. They can sing the song as they go around the first time; then the music can quicken up while they go around again, gradually slowing up as the merry-go-round comes to a halt.

Ah! si mon moine vou— -lait dan- ser, Ah! si mon moine vou— -
Oh! if my top will— dance with me, Oh! if my top will—

lait dan - ser, Un ca - pu - chon je lui don - ne - rais, Un
dance with me, So ve - ry hap - py—— I shall be, So

ca - pu - chon je lui don - ne - rais. Dan - se, mon moine, dan - se. Tu
ve - ry hap - py—— I shall be. Dance, my top, come dance now;

n'en - tends pas la dan - se. Tu n'en - tends pas mon mou -
Spin a - round, a - round now. I love my top to——

lin lon là! Tu n'en - tends pas mon mou - lin mar - cher.
dance with me; He spins a - round so——— mer - ri - ly.

Ah! if my monk will dance,
Ah! if my monk will dance,
I will give him a hood (cowl),
I will give him a hood.
Dance, my monk, dance.
You don't { know how to dance.
{ hear the dance
You don't hear my mill
You don't hear how my mill turns on.

The Merry-Go-Round
Oh! off we go on the merry-go-round,
Oh! off we go on the merry-go-round.
Our feet can scarcely touch the ground

As we go whirling round and round.
Gee up, horsie, whoa there!
We love to ride on the merry-go-round.
It's quite the nicest thing in town.

The Top
Oh! if my top will dance with me,
Oh! if my top will dance with me,
So very happy I shall be,
So very happy I shall be.
Dance, my top, come dance now;
Spin around, around now.
I love my top to dance with me;
He spins around so merrily.

Alouette!

Je t'y plumerai: I will pluck your . . .

cou: *neck* →
bec: *beak*
dos: *back* →

Like other cumulative fun songs, "Alouette" has a phrase added to the verse each time you sing it. The chorus echoes the solo singer. There are a number of verses and you can add more, as long as the soloist can remember them.

This is an obvious solo (teacher) and chorus (children) song with appropriate actions.

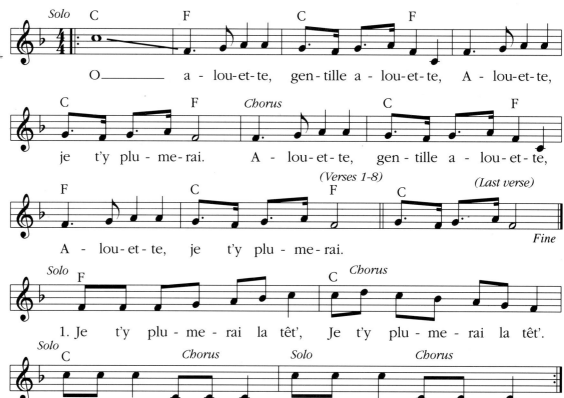

Solo

O——— a - lou-et-te, gen-tille a-lou-et-te, A-lou-et-te,

je t'y plu-me-rai. A-lou-et-te, gen-tille a-lou-et-te,

(Verses 1-8) *(Last verse)*

A-lou-et-te, je t'y plu-me-rai. *Fine*

Solo *Chorus*

1. Je t'y plu-me-rai la têt', Je t'y plu-me-rai la têt'.

Solo *Chorus* *Solo* *Chorus*

Et la têt', Et la têt', A-lou-ett' A-lou-ett'.

têt(e): *head*
nez: *nose*
yeux: *eyes*
pattes: *feet*

O alouette, gentille alouette,
Alouette, je t'y plumerai.
Alouette, gentille alouette,
Alouette, je t'y plumerai.
1. Je t'y plumerai la têt',
   Je t'y plumerai la têt'.
   Et la têt', et la têt',
   Alouett'
   Alouett'.

2. Je t'y plumerai le bec
3. Je t'y plumerai le nez
4. Je t'y plumerai les yeux
5. Je t'y plumerai le cou
6. Je t'y plumerai le dos
7. Je t'y plumerai les patt's.

En roulant ma boule

The early explorers sang while they paddled Canada's rivers, in order to keep together and to stay alert on their long canoe voyages. They therefore needed songs with a great many verses, and ones that had a verse and a chorus, so that those who did not know the verse could at least join in to sing the chorus. The men singing this song were French explorers, or coureurs-de-bois, who adopted an old fifteenth century French song with a catchy tune, probably changing or adding to the words as they felt inclined.

"En roulant" is a good practice song for the French "en" sound. The children enjoy throwing an imaginary or real ball to this little chorus.

"See the Leaves" is the chorus of this song. As it has such a catchy tune for doing things to, it could also be sung as a leaf-raking autumn song. It is fun to use real leaves and have the children listen to the sound that they make. You could make up additional words which would suit snow-shovelling or some other activity.

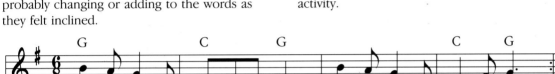

En rou-lant ma   bou-le rou-lant.   En rou-lant ma   bou - le.
On, roll on, my   ball,— roll on;   On, roll on, my   ball, roll on.

Fine

See the Leaves
See, the leaves are falling down,
Red and yellow, gold and brown.
See them twist and turn around
As they flutter to the ground.
Let us sweep them into a pile,
Rustling, rustling, all the while.
As they lie upon the ground
Still they make a rustling sound.

Our Toboggan

The opening verses of the French words that go with this melody describe the fun that boys and girls have together when they are young, but later verses paint a very gloomy picture of what happens to them when they grow up and get married. Because the gloomy words do not seem to fit this lively melody, the song is not often sung. New words can be sung to the tune, which obviously suits some kind of open air activity such as tobogganning. You can probably think of still other activities to sing about, and make up your own words to fit this melody.

This song can be learned unaccompanied by action, and when the children know it they can dramatize it. Please note the built-in discipline of "stop, stop, stop" *before* they tumble onto the ground! Most easily played outside, this song needs lots of space.

French folk melody, "Dans tous les cantons."

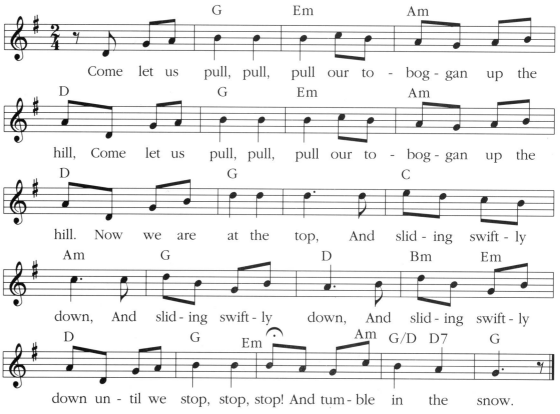

Come let us pull, pull, pull our to - bog - gan up the hill, Come let us pull, pull, pull our to - bog - gan up the hill. Now we are at the top, And slid - ing swift - ly down, And slid - ing swift - ly down, And slid - ing swift - ly down un - til we stop, stop, stop! And tum - ble in the snow.

La poulette grise

This is a French Canadian lullaby (probably originally French) about hens of different colours. Only a few of Alan Mills's suggested verses are here; the singers may have the fun of making up additional ones. The trick, of course, is to match the colour word with a rhyming word.

Alan has changed the style of the verse in the English version so that rhymes may fit in more easily. As it is a lullaby and babies sometimes take a long while to go to sleep, any number of verses may be added.

C'est la pou-let-te gri-se Qui pond dans l'é - gli-se.
There is a grey hen, ba-by, In the church, my ba-by.

Ell' va pon - dre un pet - it co - co Pour son p'tit qui va
She will lay a pret-ty lit - tle egg Just for you if you'll

fair' do - di - che; Ell' va pon - dre un pet - it co - co
go to sleep. She will lay a pret - ty lit - tle egg

Pour son p'tit qui va fair' do - do. Do - di - che, do - do.
Just for you if you'll go to sleep. Sleep now, my ba - by.

C'est la poulette grise
Qui pond dans l'église.
Ell' va pondre un petit coco
Pour son p'tit qui va fair' dodiche;
Ell' va pondre un petit coco
Pour son p'tit qui va fair' dodo.
Dodiche, dodo.

C'est la poulette brune
Qui pond dans la lune.

C'est la poulette blanche
Qui pond dans les branches.

There is a grey hen, baby,
In the church, my baby.
She will lay a pretty little egg
Just for you if you'll go to sleep;
She will lay a pretty little egg
Just for you if you'll go to sleep.
Sleep now, my baby.

There is a brown hen, baby,
In the town, my baby.

There is a white hen, baby
In the light, my baby.

Gai lon la, gai le rosier

This French song has become well known in Canada because of its charming melody. It describes a visit to an aunt in the country. In the first verse we have the original French words, which mention a bird that does not exist in Canada. (You might be able to listen to a record of the nightingale's beautiful song.) In place of the many remaining verses, which tell what an adult would do at this cottage in France, here are two other verses describing what a Canadian child would do if visiting an aunt in her Canadian cottage.

After the whole song has been sung once, each verse can be used for movement, verse one "wandering in the wood and listening to the birds," verse two "skating" and verse three "swimming." Part of the class can sing while the others move, or the song can be played on the piano or autoharp.

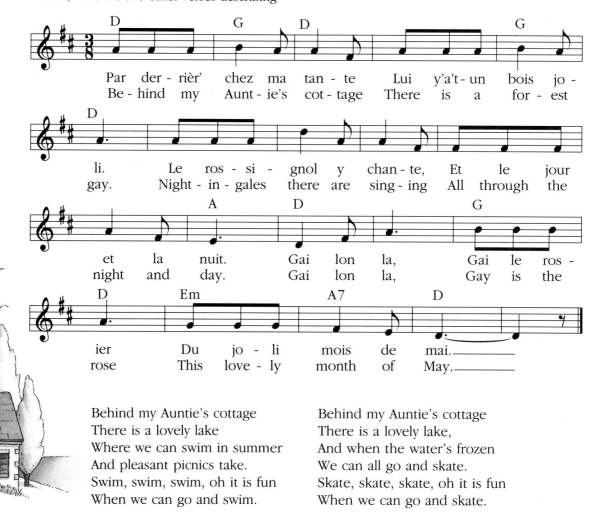

Par der - rièr' chez ma tan - te Lui y'a t - un bois jo - li.
Be - hind my Aunt - ie's cot - tage There is a for - est gay.

Le ros - si - gnol y chan - te, Et le jour et la nuit.
Night - in - gales there are sing - ing All through the night and day.

Gai lon la, Gai le ros - ier Du jo - li mois de mai.
Gai lon la, Gay is the rose This love - ly month of May.

Behind my Auntie's cottage
There is a lovely lake
Where we can swim in summer
And pleasant picnics take.
Swim, swim, swim, oh it is fun
When we can go and swim.

Behind my Auntie's cottage
There is a lovely lake,
And when the water's frozen
We can all go and skate.
Skate, skate, skate, oh it is fun
When we can go and skate.

Iroquois Lullaby

This lullaby can be sung in Iroquois, English or French. Alan Mills, who has collected and sung many Canadian folk songs, was the first to write it down. It was sung to him by the Iroquois of Caughnawaga, which is on the south side of the St. Lawrence just west of Montreal.

Although lullabies should be unaccompanied (can you imagine a mother playing an instrument while she lulls her baby?) a slow drum beat goes well with this lullaby. If the group sings the Iroquois, English and French versions in succession, three children can have a turn on the drum.

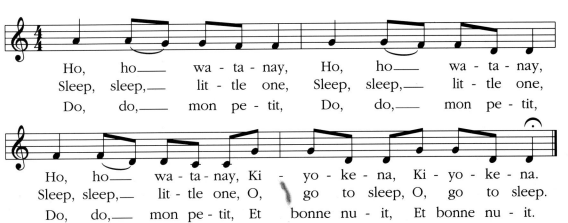

Ho,   ho—   wa - ta - nay,   Ho,   ho—   wa - ta - nay,
Sleep, sleep,— lit - tle one,   Sleep, sleep,— lit - tle one,
Do,   do,—   mon pe - tit,   Do,   do,—   mon pe - tit,

Ho,   ho—   wa - ta - nay, Ki - yo - ke - na, Ki - yo - ke - na.
Sleep, sleep,— lit - tle one, O,   go   to sleep, O,   go   to sleep.
Do,   do,—   mon pe - tit, Et bonne nu - it, Et bonne nu - it.

Blood on the Saddle

Here is a very bloody cowboys' song which describes a rodeo accident. The scene described is rather gruesome, but the song seems to have been sung with great gusto and quite a lot of enjoyment, as if the tale were never intended to be taken too seriously.

Although this song may have come originally from Arizona, a Dr. E.A. Corbett remembers hearing it sung in Calgary as early as 1905.

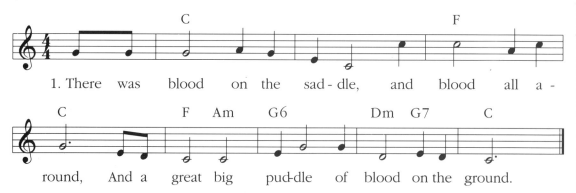

1. There was blood on the sad-dle, and blood all a-round, And a great big pud-dle of blood on the ground.

2. The cowboy lay in it
All covered with gore,
And he won't go riding
No broncos no more.

3. O pity the cowboy
All bloody and red,
For his bronco fell on him
And mashed in his head.

Bonhomm', Bonhomm'

"Bonhomme" did not originate in French-speaking Canada, but is very popular there. Like the other cumulative song "Alouette," it is very easy to sing in the original tongue, so try it in French even though the English words are given.

The soloist introduces one instrument after another, mimicking its sound in the "zing, zing, zing" line and miming the action of playing it. The chorus echoes the soloist. Any number of instruments can be added or substituted for the ones mentioned here. It is a good way of getting to know the names of musical instruments in French.

Solo G C *Chorus*

Bon - homm', Bon homm', sais - tu jou - er? Bon - homm', Bon -
Good friend, good friend, say, can you play? Good friend, good

Am D *Solo* G

homm', sais - tu jou - er? Sais - tu jou - er de ce vio - lon -
friend, say, can you play___ the vi - o -

C *Chorus* Am D *Solo* D

là? Sais - tu jou - er de ce vio - lon - là? Zing, zing,
lin? Say, can you play___ the vi - o - lin? Zing, zing,

D G D *Chorus* G D *(Solo~last time)*

zing de ce vio - lon - là! Zing, zing, zing de ce vio - lon - là! Bon -
zing on the vi - o - lin! Zing, zing, zing on the vi - o - lin! Good

D7 *(Chorus)* G C

homm', *(Bon-homm')* Tu n'est pas maîtr' dans ta mai -
friend, *(Bon-homm')* You are not boss in your own

D C D G

son, Quand nous y som - mes.___
house When we come here to play.

17

The final "Bonhomm'" can also be sung with solo and chorus if wanted, i.e.

Solo:	Bonhomm', Bonhomm', sais-tu jouer?	Good friend, good friend, say, can you play?
Chorus:	Bonhomm', Bonhomm', sais-tu jouer?	Good friend, good friend, say, can you play?
Solo:	Sais-tu jouer de ce violon-là?	Say, can you play the violin?
Chorus:	Sais-tu jouer de ce violon-là?	Say, can you play the violin?
Solo:	Zing, zing, zing de ce violon-là!	Zing, zing, zing on the violin!
Chorus:	Zing, zing, zing de ce violon-là!	Zing, zing, zing on the violin!
	Bonhomm',	Good friend,
	Tu n'est pa maîtr' dans ta maison,	You are not boss in your own house
	Quand nous y sommes.	When we come here to play.

Second Soloist:	Bonhomm', Bonhomm', sais-tu jouer?	Good friend, good friend, say can you play?
Chorus:	Bonhomm', Bonhomm', sais-tu jouer?	Good friend, good friend, say can you play?
Second Soloist:	Sais-tu jouer de ce flûte-là?	Say, can you play on the little flute?
Chorus:	Sais-tu jouer de ce flûte-là?	Say, can you play on the little flute?
Second Soloist:	Flût', flût', flût' de cett' flût' qui flûte!	Floo, floo, floo on the little flute!
Chorus:	Flût', flût', flût' de cett' flût' qui flûte!	Floo, floo, floo on the little flute!
First Soloist:	Zing, zing, zing de ce violon-là!	Zing, zing, zing on the violin!
Chorus:	Zing, zing, zing de ce violon-là!	Zing, zing, zing on the violin'
	Bonhomm'!	Good friend,
	Tu n'est pas maîtr' dans ta maison,	You are not boss in your own house
	Quand nous y sommes!	When we come here to play

Third Soloist:	Bonhomm', Bonhomm', sais-tu jouer?	Good friend, good friend, say can you play?
Chorus:	Bonhomm', Bonhomm', sais-tu jouer?	Good friend, good friend, say can you play?
Third Soloist:	Sais-tu jouer de ce tambour-là?	Say, can you play on the big bass drum?
Chorus:	Sais-tu jouer de ce tambour-là?	Say, can you play on the big bass drum?
Third Soloist:	Boom, boom, boom de ce tambour-là!	Boom, boom, boom on the big bass drum!
Chorus:	Boom, boom, boom de ce tambour-là!	Boom, boom, boom on the big bass drum!
Second Soloist:	Flût', flût', flût' de cett' flût' qui flûte!	Floo, floo, floo on the little flute!
Chorus:	Flût', flût', flût' de cett' flût' qui flûte!	Floo, floo, floo on the little flute!
First Soloist:	Zing, zing, zing de ce violon-là!	Zing, zing, zing on the violin!
Chorus:	Zing, zing, zing de ce violon-là!	Zing, zing, zing on the violin!
	Bonhomm'!	Good friend,
	Tu n'est pas maîtr' dans ta maison,	You are not boss in your own house
	Quand nous y sommes!	When we come here to play.

Donkey Riding

This song is not about the thistle-eating, braying kind of donkey, but about the mechanical kind which powered the winch on cargo boats; this was called a "donkey engine." The song was sung by sailors to keep themselves happy and working together while they loaded up the boat. As you see, the cargo was timber (wood) from Quebec, which was taken from the port of Quebec to the port of Cardiff, Wales. (Originally these ships sailed from Glasgow and Liverpool, ports in Scotland and England.)

Because the men thought that they were well paid, they sang about "a king with a golden crown." The cargo boats travelled very slowly, so the sailors came home with "three months pay," which must have seemed quite a lot of money.

In order to sing this song as the sailors did, it is important to keep the time and rhythm very exact. "Donkey Riding" sounds excellent if arranged for percussion instruments.

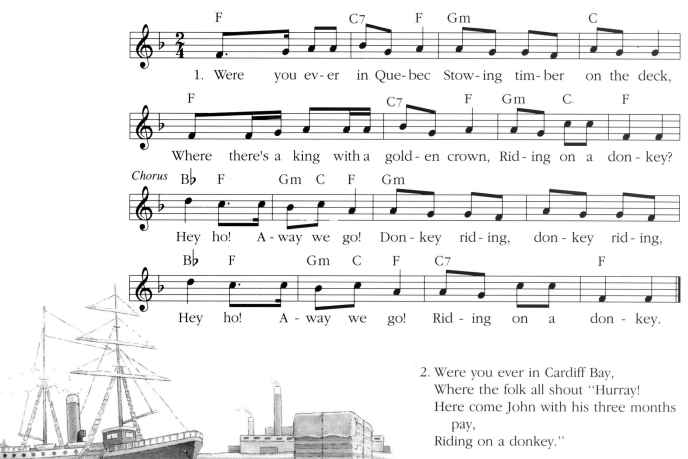

1. Were you ev-er in Que-bec Stow-ing tim-ber on the deck,
Where there's a king with a gold-en crown, Rid-ing on a don-key?

Chorus
Hey ho! A-way we go! Don-key rid-ing, don-key rid-ing,
Hey ho! A-way we go! Rid-ing on a don-key.

2. Were you ever in Cardiff Bay,
   Where the folk all shout "Hurray!
   Here come John with his three months pay,
   Riding on a donkey."

20

Inuit Lullaby

This is a lullaby which was sung by an Inuit family in Cape Dorset on the southern coast of Baffin Island. It is quite slow and needs lots of breath, so sit up tall and take a deep breath before trying to sing it. In the first bar you will notice the syncopated beat. Perhaps this lullaby would be easier to sing rhythmically if it were accompanied with a drum beat, which could be practised before you sing the song.

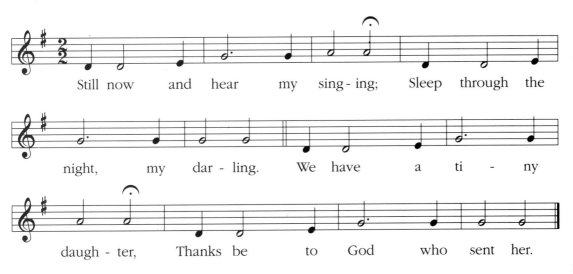

Still now and hear my sing-ing; Sleep through the
night, my dar-ling. We have a ti - ny
daugh-ter, Thanks be to God who sent her.

Though she as yet knows nothing,
She is so sweet I'm singing.
We have a tiny daughter,
Thanks be to God who sent her.

Flunky Jim

This song was sung to me in Saskatoon, Saskatchewan, by the grandson of the man—a teacher—who made it up. In the years known as the "Depression," when many people were out of work and money was very scarce, the children were given money by the government for every gopher tail that they turned in.

(Gophers ate the already scarce grain crops.) Jim was the youngest boy in this family and his father made up this song after listening to Jim bragging about the new clothes he was going to get with his gopher money. Like "I'se the B'y," this is a skipping tune.

1. I am the flun-ky of the house, They call me Flun-ky Jim.— You'll find me knock-ing a - bout the yard in a hat with-out a brim. — My o - ver-alls are shab-by and I have no shirt at all——— But I'm go - ing to get a new out-fit with my goph-er tails next fall.— *Chorus* Knock-ing a-round the yard, boys, Knock-ing a - round the yard.— It is - n't an - y ea - sy job, don't fool your-self, old pard.— My o - ver-alls are

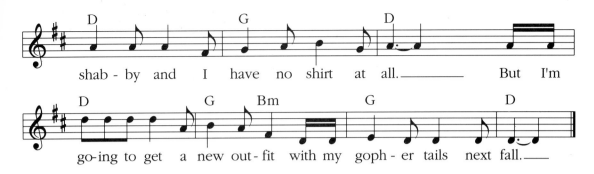

shab - by and I have no shirt at all._____ But I'm

go - ing to get a new out - fit with my goph - er tails next fall.___

2. I've counted all my gopher tails;
I've almost got enough
To buy a hat, a fancy shirt,
And pants that have a cuff.
And then I'll hand my old ones on;
They really are too small.
Oh, I'll be swell, when once I sell
My gopher tails next fall.

Icelandic Lullaby

As you probably know, there are many Icelandic Canadians; most live in Manitoba and Saskatchewan. As most Icelandic families still speak Icelandic, this very lovely and well-known lullaby is still sung by them.

Most lullabies tell the baby to go to sleep, but this one suggests that the baby stay awake—at least long enough to see the swans fly, for according to an old Icelandic legend, when the swans fly they also sing with a sound like silver bells. Thus encouraged, Baby tries to stay awake, but the effort is too great and he promptly falls asleep, which is probably what Mother wanted all along!

Thinking of "little lambs at play" might be a baby's version of "counting sheep" in order to fall asleep.

Bi bi og bla - ka Can you see the swans fly? You
(Bye, bye and hush now)

may pre-tend to go to sleep, but I know you will want to peep.

Bi - um bi - um bam - ba Sleep, my lit - tle ba - by. You'll
(Lul - la - by my ba - by)

fall a-sleep when your thoughts stray to lit-tle lambs at play.

I'se the B'y That Builds the Boat

This song comes from Newfoundland and was made up by the men who built and sailed the fishing boats. It is a song to dance to and has a number of verses. Of these I have included only two, because the singers can make up some of their own, if any more are wanted. The three place-names (Fogo, Twillingate and Mor'ton's Harbour) are little ports around Notre Dame Bay in northwestern Newfoundland. You will notice that the sailors say "b'y" instead of "boy." You will also notice if you clap the rhythm of this song that it is a skipping tune.

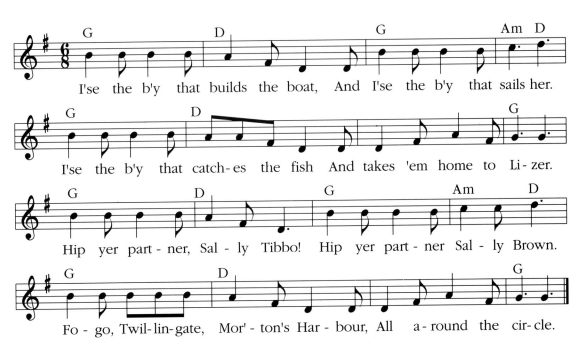

I'se the b'y that builds the boat, And I'se the b'y that sails her.

I'se the b'y that catch-es the fish And takes 'em home to Li-zer.

Hip yer part-ner, Sal-ly Tibbo! Hip yer part-ner Sal-ly Brown.

Fo-go, Twil-lin-gate, Mor'-ton's Har-bour, All a-round the cir-cle.

I don't want your maggoty fish
That's no good for winter;
I can buy as good as that
Down in Bonavista.

Jack Was Every Inch a Sailor

Jack provides us with a humorous version of "Jonah and the whale." This popular song has been sung in Newfoundland for over fifty years.

Bacalhao (pronounced Back-a-loo) is a rocky island off the east coast of Newfoundland where there is an important lighthouse. Indian Harbour, on the Labrador coast, was a well-known cod-fishing centre around the turn of the century.

This song is well travelled and better known than most of the songs in this book. Because of its lively words but somewhat monotonous tune it needs to be sung briskly and not allowed to drag.

1. Now, 'twas twen-ty five or thir-ty years since Jack first saw the light. He

came in - to this world of woe one dark and storm-y night. He was

born on board his fa-ther's ship as she was ly-ing to 'Bout

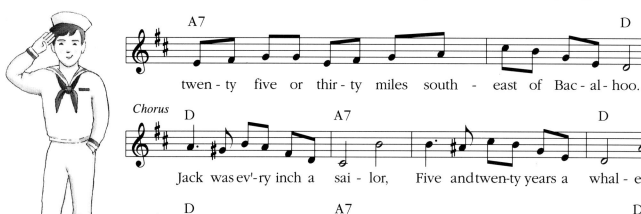

twen-ty five or thir-ty miles south - east of Bac - al - hoo.

Chorus

Jack was ev'-ry inch a sai - lor, Five and twen-ty years a whal - er,

Jack was ev'-ry inch a sai - lor, He was born up - on the bright blue sea.

2. When Jack grew up to be a man, he went
     to Labrador;
  He fished in Indian Harbour, where his
     father fished before.
  On his returning in the fog, he met a
     heavy gale,
  And Jack was swept into the sea and
     swallowed by a whale.

Chorus
  Jack was every inch a sailor,
  Five and twenty years a whaler;
  Jack was every inch a sailor,
  He was born upon the bright blue sea.

3. The whale went straight for Baffin's Bay
     'bout ninety knots an hour,
  And ev'ry time he'd blow a spray he'd
     send it in a shower.
  "Oh now," says Jack unto himself, "I
     must see what he's about";
  He caught the whale all by the tail and
     turned him inside out.

J'entends le moulin

This French song, which has been adopted by Canadians, is really two songs: the verse is one; the chorus, another. Whatever its origin, it is fun to sing, particularly in French. One can almost hear the mill wheel turning, especially if rhythm sticks or tone blocks are used for the "tique taque" part.

J'en - tends le mou - lin, ti - que, ti - que, ta - que. J'en - tends le mou - lin,

ta - que. Mon père a fait bâ - tir mai - son, J'en - tends le mou - lin,

ta - que. L'a fait bâ - tir à trois pi - gnons, Ti - que

ta - que, ti - que, ta - que, J'en - tends le mou - lin,

ti - que, ti - que, ta - que, J'en - tends le mou - lin, ta - que.

I hear the mill wheel ticker ticker tacker,
I hear the mill wheel turning.
My father builds himself a house.
I hear the mill wheel turning.

He has three carpenters to help.
Ticker tacker, ticker tacker,
I hear the mill wheel ticker ticker tacker,
I hear the mill wheel turning.

The Kangaroo

Most of us have tried the "whispering game," in which a player whispers a written message quickly to someone who in turn whispers what he has heard to someone else, and by the time it has been whispered to about ten people it often sounds nothing like the original message. Something like this has happened to "The Kangaroo," which is a very old song dating back to the sixteenth century. In the original, the "kangaroo" was a crow, which of course sounds more sensible.

The other words of the verses are fairly accurate, buy many nonsense words were needed to fill out the rest of the melody. Helen Creighton, who collected this song in Nova Scotia, must have had a difficult time deciding how to write them all out. The tune is tricky, so you may find that it takes practice to say all these nonsense sounds quickly and clearly.

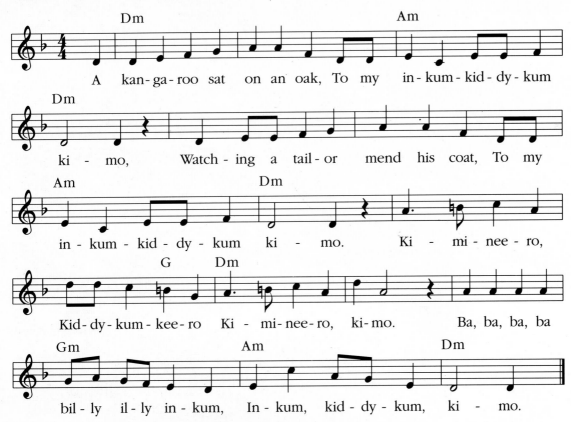

D'où viens-tu, bergère?

PART 3

This carol came from France but is sung everywhere in Canada and is regarded as French Canadian. It has a question and answer form which makes it very easy to learn. As you are likely to sing the Huron carol in translation, this carol ought to be sung in French.

1. D'où viens -tu ber - gè - re, D'où viens - tu?

D'où viens -tu ber - gè - re, D'où viens - tu?

Je viens de l'é - ta - ble De m'y pro - me - ner.

J'ai vu un mi - ra - cle ce soir ar - ri - vé.

2. Qu'as-tu vu, bergère, } *repeat*
   Qu'as-tu vu?
   "J'ai vu dans la crèche
   Un petit enfant
   Sur la paille fraîche
   Mis bien tendrement."

3. Est'il beau, bergère, } *repeat*
   Est'il beau?
   "Plus beau que la lune,
   Aussi le soleil.
   Jamais dans le monde
   On vit son pareil."

Whence come you, shepherd maiden?

1. Whence, O shepherd maiden, } *repeat*
   Whence come you?
   "I come from the stable
   Where this very night
   Mine eyes have been dazzled
   By a wond'rous sight."

2. What saw you, O maiden, } *repeat*
   What saw you?
   "There within the manger
   A little child I saw,
   Sweetly he lay sleeping
   On the fresh-piled straw."

3. Was he fair, O maiden, } *repeat*
   Was he fair?
   "Fairer than the moon is;
   Fairer than the sun.
   Never in the world was
   Such a lovely one."

The Huron Carol

This song is really the first Canadian Christmas carol, as it was written in the Huron language to a french tune. The writer was probably Father Jean Brébeuf, a Jesuit missionary who lived and worked with the Hurons, from 1626 to 1649. When the Hurons were attacked by the Iroquois, the survivors fled, some going to live in Lorette near Quebec City. They must have continued to sing this song, for later it was translated into French by another Jesuit priest, Father de Villeneuve, under the title "*Jésus est né.*" In 1926 a Canadian poet, J.E. Middleton, wrote the very beautiful English words, which are an interpretation rather than a literal translation. Because these words not only fit the melody very well but also seem to capture the feeling of a native carol, they deserve first preference for singing.

1. 'Twas in the moon of win-ter-time, when all the birds had fled, That might-y Git-chi-Man-i-tou sent an-gel choirs in-stead. Be - fore their light the stars grew dim, and wan-d'ring hun-ters heard the hymn___ Je-sus, your king is born, Je-sus is born, In ex - cel - sis glo - ri - a!

2. Within a lodge of broken bark
The tender babe was found.
A ragged robe of rabbit skin
Enwrapped his beauty round,
And as the hunter braves drew nigh
The angel song rang loud and high.
"Jesus, your king, is born,
Jesus is born,
In excelsis gloria."

Jésus est né
Chrétiens, prenez courage,
Jésus Sauveur est né.
Du malin les ouvrages
A jamais sont ruinés.
Quand il chante merveille
A ces troublants appas
Ne prêtez plus l'oreille.
"Jésus est né,
In excelsis gloria."

Haul on the Bowline

Like "Donkey Riding," this is a sea shanty; sailors sang it to pace their work as they hauled on a rope together. It was originally sung by British sailors, and was passed on by early British explorers to Canadian seamen. The Canadians sang it not only at sea but also when they sailed on the Great Lakes.

The bowline, pronounced "bo'lin," was a very important rope on the early square-rigged sailing ships. It was fastened to the edge of the sail so that men could haul on it to flatten the sail and get the cutting edge into the wind. Later, when the design of sailing ships was changed, this line became less important; however, the song was still sung when a short, hard pull was needed.

To see how useful this sort of song was, pretend that you are pulling on a rope and giving your hardest pull on the word "haul."

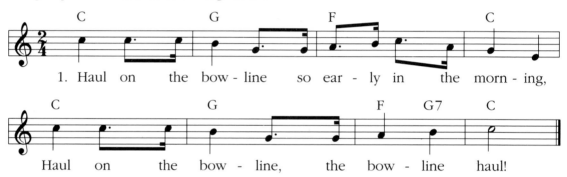

1. Haul on the bow-line so ear-ly in the morn-ing,
Haul on the bow-line, the bow-line haul!

2. Haul on the bowline,
Kitty is me darling.
Haul on the bowline,
The bowline *haul*.

3. Haul on the bowline,
Our bully ship's a-rolling
Haul on the bowline,
The bowline *haul*.

Klondike

This song grew out of the gold rush excitement which started in 1896 with the discovery of gold in the Yukon, an area east of the Yukon River, whose principal town was Dawson. The economic depression of the 1890s still gripped the Northwest, and the gold rush business helped to get things moving again in Seattle, Victoria and Vancouver. Moodyville was the old millsite waterfront area of the growing North Vancouver.

"Klondike" might well have begun its life in the music halls or bars. Or it could have started as a musical advertisement of gear for the Klondike, for in Vancouver, outfitters actually had parades of mules loaded with a miner's complete equipment and bedecked with the names of the companies selling the goods. Whatever its origin, it is a lively tune full of a probably unjustified, but contagious, optimism!

P.J. Thomas Collection

1. Oh, come to the place where they struck it rich, Come where the trea-sure lies hid!__ Where your hat full of mud is a five-pound note And a clod on your heel is a quid! Klon-dike! Klon-dike! Oh, lab-el your lug-gage for Klon-dike. Oh, there ain't no luck in the town to-day; There ain't no work__ down Mood-y-ville way. So pack up your traps and be off, I say, Off and a-way to the Klon-dike!

2. Oh, they scratches the earth and it tumbles out,
   More than your hands can hold;
   For the hills above and the plains beneath
   Are crackin' and bustin' with gold!

35

Lots of Fish in Bonavist' Harbour

Here is a Newfoundland fishing song which points out that Carbonear, the largest town in Conception Bay just west of St. John's, provides a large number of men to help with the fishing. It was probably sung when they had caught a great many fish and were feeling ready for square dancing.

Oh! there's lots of fish in Bon-a-vist' har-bour, Lots of fish right in a-round here. Boys and girls are fish-ing to-geth-er, For-ty-five from Car-bon-ear.___ Oh!___ Catch-a-hold this one, catch-a-hold that one, Swing a-round this one, dance a-round she. Catch-a-hold this one, catch-a-hold that one, Did-dle-dum this one, did-dle-dum dee.___

A Paper of Pins

Here is a love song with a funny twist, which I'm sure the boys will enjoy. This song lends itself to acting, so why not divide into "men" and "women" and see what you can do.

This version of the song was collected by Kenneth Peacock from Joshua Osborn of Seal Cove, White Bay, Newfoundland.

I'll give to you a pa - per of pins; It is the way my love be - gins, If you might mar - ry me, me, me, If you might mar - ry me.

Man

1. I'll give to you a paper of pins;
   It is the way my love begins,
   If you might marry me, me, me,
   If you might marry me.

3. I'll give to you a suit of red,
   Stitched around with golden thread.
   If you . . .

5. I'll give to you a cloak of green,
   To make you look like a fairy queen. . . .

7. I'll give to you the keys to my heart,
   Locked in love and never to part. . . .

9. I'll give to you the keys of my chest,
   And plenty of money at my request. . . .

11. Poor foolish girl, don't think it's so,
    It's only a joke from me, you know.
    Sure I wouldn't marry you, you, you,
    Sure I wouldn't marry you!

Woman

2. I won't accept your paper of pins
   If that's the way your love begins.
   Sure I won't marry you, you, you,
   Sure I won't marry you.

4. I won't accept your suit of red,
   Stitched around with golden thread.
   Sure I won't . . .

6. I won't accept your cloak of green,
   To make me look like a fairy queen. . .

8. I won't accept the keys to your heart,
   Locked in love and never to part. . . .

10. I will accept the keys of your chest
    With plenty of money at my request,
    And I will marry you, you, you,
    And I will marry you.

The Sailor's Alphabet

If you are fond of sailing or sea lore, you will enjoy this descriptive list of terms used by the crews of the old sailing ships. Besides helping the seamen to pull on ropes or haul up the anchor, such a song could spur new members of the crew into learning and understanding ship's jargon. It might be a good idea to make up your own alphabet when you want to remember certain things.

Most of the terms are self-explanatory. For the ones which may be new to you, here are a few definitions.

Capstan: The anchor cable is wound around the capstan, and it took a team of men to push the capstan bars like a turnstile to make the capstan rotate. This work led to the singing of a fairly long and continuous song which was called a capstan shanty—or a capstan-and-windlass shanty if it accompanied pulling on the windlass.

Davit: Small boats such as lifeboats are slung from davits.

Hawser: A very thick, strong rope. In very early shipbuilding days it acted as a support for the hull of the ship in drydock.

Stuns'l boom: The boom of the studding sail, which is held by the irons.

Jib boom: A spar projecting forward from the bow.

Keelsons: Timbers bolted inside the hull to the keel to give the hull strength, especially where the keel curves most.

Lanyards: The stays and shrouds which support the masts are stretched by the lanyards.

Quadrant: A navigation instrument for determining position.

Windlass: The anchor winch.

P.J. Thomas Collection

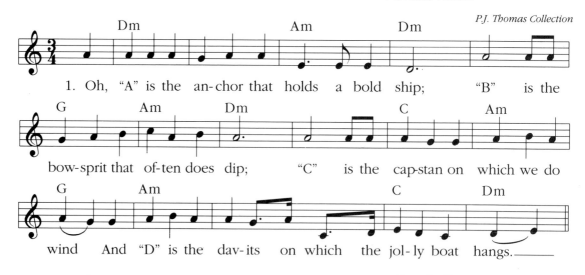

1. Oh, "A" is the an-chor that holds a bold ship; "B" is the bow-sprit that of-ten does dip; "C" is the cap-stan on which we do wind And "D" is the dav-its on which the jol-ly boat hangs.____

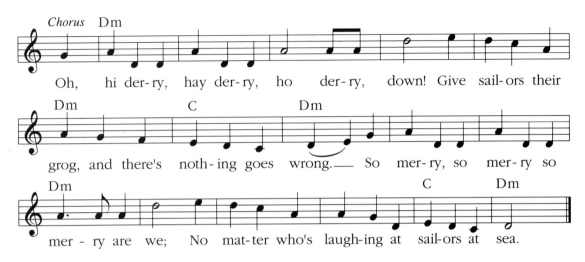

Chorus Dm

Oh, hi der-ry, hay der-ry, ho der-ry, down! Give sail-ors their

Dm · · · C · · · Dm

grog, and there's noth-ing goes wrong.— So mer-ry, so mer-ry so

Dm · · · · · · · · · C · · · Dm

mer - ry are we; No mat-ter who's laugh-ing at sail-ors at sea.

2. "E" is the ensign, the red, white and
   blue;
   "F" is the fo'c'sle, holds the ship's crew,
   "G" is the gangway on which the mate
   takes his stand,
   And "H" is the hawser that seldom does
   strand.

3. "I" is the irons where the stuns'l boom
   sits;
   "J" is the jib boom that often does dip;
   "K" is the keelsons of which you've
   heard told,
   And "L" are the lanyards that always will
   hold.

4. "M" is the main mast so stout and so
   strong;
   "N" is the needle that never points
   wrong;
   "O" are the orders of which we must be
   ware,

And "P" are the pumps that cause sailors
to swear.

5. "Q" is the quadrant, the sun for to take;
   "R" is the riggin' that always does shake;
   "S" is the starboard side of our bold
   ship,
   And "T" are the topmasts that often do
   split.

6. "U" is the ugliest old Captain of all;
   "V" is the vapour that comes with the
   squall;
   "W" is the windlass on which we do
   wind,
   And "X," "Y," and "Z," well I can't put
   in rhyme.

Sioux Lullaby

This lullaby was sung to me in Saskatchewan by a Sioux friend called Dorothy Frances. We tried to write out the words in the Sioux language, and although this is what they sound like, I am not at all sure that we spelled them correctly. Anyway, Dorothy's version enables you to sing the words in Sioux as well as in English and French. To help keep the rhythm, which is not easy, try accompanying the song with a quiet drum beat.

Song of Louis Riel

Louis Riel was thought to have written this song, and since we know that he made up verses and poems all his life, it is possible that he composed these verses (or ones like them) when he was in prison, and handed them on to his friends. His story, which is also the story of the Prairie Métis, is a fascinating one, and I hope that this song increases the singers' interest in it.

After their defeat in battle, many of the Manitoba Métis settled in Lebret, Saskatchewan, where I collected this song. It was sung to me by Joseph Gaspard Jeannotte, one of the Métis living there, and before he started it he expressed his admiration for their hero, Louis Riel.

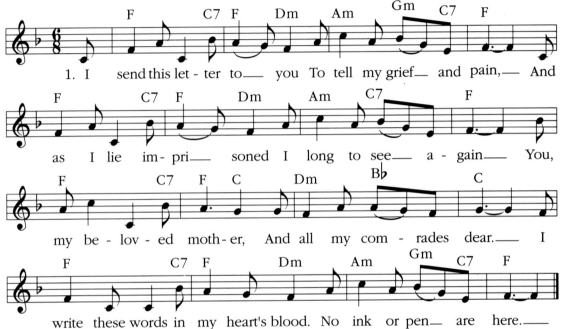

1. I send this let-ter to— you To tell my grief— and pain,— And as I lie im-pri— soned I long to see— a-gain— You, my be-lov-ed moth-er, And all my com-rades dear.— I write these words in my heart's blood. No ink or pen— are here.—

2. My friends in arms and children,
   Please weep and pray for me;
   I fought to keep our country
   So that we might be free.
   When you receive this letter,
   Please weep for me and pray
   That I may die with bravery
   Upon that fearful day.

1. C'est au champ de bataille,
   J'ai fait crier mes douleurs,
   Où tout 'cun doute se passe
   Ça fait frémir les coeurs.

   Or je r'çois-t-une lettre
   De ma chère maman.
   J'avais ni plum' ni encre.
   Pour pouvoir lui écrire.

2. Or je pris mon canif,
   Je le trempai dans mon sang,
   Pour écrir'-t-une lettre
   A ma chère maman.
   Quand ell' r'çevra cett' lettre
   Toute écrit' de sang,
   Ses yeux baignant de larmes,
   Son coeur s'allant mourant.

3. S'y jette à genoux par terre
   En appelant ses enfants:
   Priez pour votr' p'tit frère
   Qui est au régiment.
   Mourir, c'est pour mourir,
   Chacun meurt à son tour;
   J'aim' mieux mourir en brave,
   Faut tous mourir un jour.

Song of the Rabbit & Song of the Seagull

These two songs, which are much easier to sing than most Inuit music, reflect the life and thinking of a people who speak of nature not as scientists but only as it is related to their way of life. They have developed a detailed knowledge of animals and birds because they must hunt to live, and they realize that in order to know what a bird or animal is going to do you must know what it thinks.

Often animal behaviour is likened in Inuit art to human thinking; for example, in "Song of the Rabbit" the little rabbit too is imagined hunting as the Inuit do. Perhaps because seagulls are not valuable as food, they are seen as just part of the landscape, "eating and drifting."

Musically, as their collector Beverly Cavanagh points out, the songs have great variation in phrase length and a free rhythmic style. The final notes are very short, often followed by a hearty laugh.

The translations are not literal, but convey the sense of the original. The Inuit words have been included for both songs, and can be sung phonetically. "Song of the Seagull" suggests the rise and fall of the waves, and sounds very lovely played on a recorder or other simple woodwind instrument.

Song of the Rabbit

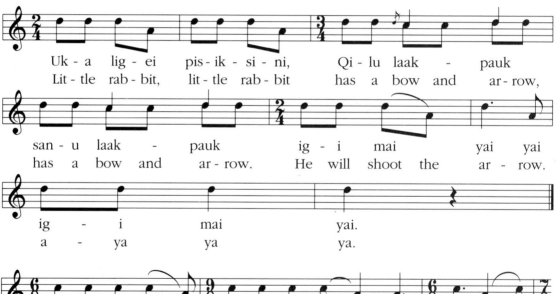

Uk - a lig - ei pis - ik - si - ni, Qi - lu laak - pauk
Lit - tle rab - bit, lit - tle rab - bit has a bow and ar - row,

san - u laak - pauk ig - i mai yai yai
has a bow and ar - row. He will shoot the ar - row.

ig - i mai yai.
a - ya ya ya.

Song of the Seagull

Na - ja - na qut___ Ni - ri - jut quu - qa - ni, Sak___
Sea - gulls are drift - ing, eat - ing and drift - ing, drift - ing. Fly - ing,

wat - suk - lu - tit ni - ri - jut___ Na - ja - na qut___ ni - ri - jut.___
fly - ing and drift - ing, eat - ing, eat - ing. Sea - gulls are drift - ing, eat - ing, drift - ing.

Way Up the Ucletaw

Here is a lumbermen's song made up in Vancouver about 1896, when there was a good deal of hardship among labourers, and a small tent town near False Creek was filled with unemployed hand loggers.

This song describes how loggers had to go up the treacherous winding part of the Seymour Narrows between Quadra and Sonora Islands known as the Yuc'ta (Yuculta) Rapids to find the pitchbacks: Douglas fir over six feet in diameter and over two hundred feet high. Heavy sap accumulated under the bark near the base of these giant trees, making it impossible to cut the bark. To get above this pitch layer or a flared butt (or if the ground was very uneven) the axemen had to fit spring boards into the bark. They then had a flat but not very safe base to stand on while they chopped. There are few—if any—of these trees left now, and in the day of the power saw it is hard to imagine how the men ever managed to fell them with their hand tools, working as they did under difficult and dangerous conditions.

P.J. Thomas Collection

1. Come, all you bull-necked log-gers,— And hear me sing my song,— For it is ve-ry short And it will not keep you long.—

Chorus
We had blan-kets for to trav-el,— Bis-cuits for to chaw.— We were in search of pitch-backs 'Way up the Uc-le-taw.—

2. We're leaving Vancouver
   With sorrow, grief and woe,
   Heading up the country
   A hundred miles or so.

3. We hired fourteen loggers,
   And we hired a man to saw.
   We had a greenhorn cook,
   And he run the hotcakes raw.

SONGS WITHOUT WORDS

Here are five songs which can be used for movement, to illustrate different time patterns or to express different moods. Three of them are very lively, and "She's Like the Swallow" and "Un Canadien errant" have beautiful, slow-moving melodies.

Vive la Canadienne

Zing, Zing, Zing

Un Canadien errant

Rattle on the Stovepipe

She's Like the Swallow

ACKNOWLEDGEMENTS

"Acadian Lullaby" and "The Kangaroo": with kind permission of the collector, Helen Creighton.

"Bonhomm' Bonhomm'": Alan Mills, *Chanton un peu*, Berandol Music Ltd., Scarborough, Ontario. With kind permission from Alan Mills.

"Donkey Riding": collected by Thomas Wood, *Oxford Song Book 2*, Oxford University Press, Oxford, England.

"Inuit Lullaby": collected by D. H. Whitbread; published by Edith Fowke and Richard Johnston, *More Folk Songs of Canada*. With kind permission from Waterloo Music Co. Ltd., Waterloo, Ontario.

"Flunky Jim," "Sioux Lullaby" and "Song of Louis Riel": collected by Barbara Cass-Beggs, *Folk Songs of Saskatchewan*, Folkways Ethnic Library F W 4312, New York, U.S.A.

"Haul on the Bowline": Elizabeth B. Greenleaf and Grace Y. Mansfield, *Ballads and Sea Songs of Newfoundland*, Harvard University Press, Cambridge, U.S.A.

"Icelandic Lullaby": collected by Horpuhl Jomar, *Islenz Songlog*. First published by Fjorar Karlmannar and Sigfus Einarsson, Reykjavik, 1905. From Department of Icelandic Literature, University of Manitoba, Winnipeg, Manitoba.

"Iroquois Lullaby": Edith Fowke, Helmut Blume, Alan Mills, *Canada's Story in Song*, W. J. Gage Ltd. Reprinted by permission of Gage Educational Publishing Ltd., Agincourt, Ontario.

"I'se the B'y that Builds the Boat," "Lots of Fish in Bonavist' Harbour" and "A Paper of Pins": collected by Kenneth Peacock, Information Canada, Ottawa, Ontario. With kind permission of the collector and Information Canada.

"Jack Was Every Inch a Sailor": *Old Time Songs and Poetry of Newfoundland*, Gerald S. Doyle Ltd., St. John's, Newfoundland, with kind permission.

"Klondike" and "The Sailor's Alphabet": sung by Captain Charles Cates. "Way Up the Ucletaw": sung by Ed Dalby. From the Phil Thomas collection, Vancouver, British Columbia. With kind permission of the collector.

"La poulette grise": Alan Mills, *Favourite French Folk Songs*, Embassy Music Corp., New York, U.S.A.

"Rattle on the Stovepipe": collected by Edith Fowke; published by Edith Fowke and Richard Johnston, *More Folk Songs of Canada*. With kind permission from Waterloo Music Ltd., Waterloo, Ontario.

"She's Like the Swallow": Maud Karpeles, *Folk Songs of Newfoundland*, reprinted by permission of Faber and Faber Ltd., London, England.

"Song of the Rabbit" and "Song of the Seagull": collected by Beverly Cavanagh. With kind permission of the collector.

"Zing, Zing, Zing": collected by S. J. Germain Lemieux, *Chansonnier franco-ontarien 1*, La Société historique du Nouvel-Ontario, Sudbury, Ontario. With kind permission of the collector.

The main reference for the following songs is Ernest Gagnon's *Chansons populaires du Canada*, Editions Beauchemin, Montreal, Québec, 1865:
"Ah! Si mon moine voulait danser!"
"Dans tous les cantons"
"D'où viens-tu, bergère?"
"En roulant ma boule"
"Gai lon la, gai le rosier"
"The Huron Carol"
"Un Canadien errant"
"Vive la Canadienne"

TRANSLATIONS

"Acadian Lullaby": Barbara Cass-Beggs

"Ah! Si mon moine voulait danser!": Edith Fowke

"Gai lon la, gai le rosier": Verse one by Edith Fowke; new verses by Barbara Cass-Beggs

"Iroquois Lullaby": English by Alan Mills; French by Evy Paraskevopoulos

"La poulette grise": Alan Mills

"Bonhomm', Bonhomm'": Alan Mills

"Icelandic Lullaby": Barbara Cass-Beggs

"J'entends le moulin": Edith Fowke

"D'où viens-tu, bergere?": based on Murray Gibbon's. Verse one by Edith Fowke; verses two and three by Barbara Cass-Beggs

"The Huron Carol": English by J.E. Middleton, used by permission of the Frederick Harris Music Company, Oakville, Ontario

"Sioux Lullaby": Barbara Cass-Beggs

"Song of Louis Riel": Barbara Cass-Beggs

"Song of the Rabbit" and "Song of the Seagull": Beverly Cavanagh

Words for "The Top," "The Merry-Go-Round," "Our Toboggan" and "See the Leaves" by Barbara Cass-Beggs